I Chronicles 25 is the true foundation for all God-pleasing music ... splendid proof that music was instituted by the Spirit of God through David.

Johann Sebastian Bach.

ISBN: 978-1-63110-553-1

Introduction

The following study was extracted from Jewish literature and the original Arithmetic of Abraham. I have read many books and studies on the spiritual significance of music, none of which satisfied my curiosity as to what the Lord deems righteous, heavenly music ... until now.

The God of Israel is an alpha-numeric God. When He speaks, He speaks alpha/numerically in word-numbers.[1] Words in the Jewish Scriptures have "parallel" meanings. For example, throughout the *Tanakh* the word WISDOM is synonymous with HaShem (the Father of mercy), with Earth, with Body, with Written Law, with Time (counting), with Way, with **text**, and with the Seventh-day Sabbath; whereas, UNDERSTANDING is synonymous with the Ruach HaKodesh (the Holy Spirit of judgment), with Heaven, with Soul, with Oral Law, with Space (measuring), with Path, with **number**, and with the Lord's Festivals. These parallels are interchanged throughout the Scriptures. KNOWLEDGE is the combination of Wisdom and Understanding, Mercy and Judgment – a *these two [Father and Holy Spirit] become one* God who created all things, <u>neither of which is fully God</u>.[2]

---

[1] The Hebraic and Greek definition of "Word" is "text and calculation" – a *these two [Father and Holy Spirit] <u>become</u> one*, alpha/numeric WORD ... God. Not a *these three <u>are</u> one* god.

[2] The only "these three are one" god of the Jewish Scriptures is *Baal* – a "Father, Son, Holy Ghost" god of which <u>*each*</u> <u>person is fully god</u>!?! Paul created his own "god" in the image and likeness of *Baal*.

According to the *Midrash*, there are 50 gates of heavenly understanding. The 49th level is the music gate second only to the *Torah* whose structure personifies the "likeness" of a musical chiasm. *Torah* is to text as *Music* is to number (a *these two become one* alpha/numeric structure) – **both are of *measure* three.**

Spiritually speaking, the "measure" of *Torah* (text) is Wisdom, Understanding, and the combination of both (Knowledge); whereas, the measure of Music (number) is Psalm, Instrument, and the combination of both, Song (a biblical *chiasm*). What orders these parallels throughout the Jewish Scriptures is the "Law of Correspondence."

The biblical language of "counting and measuring" is Arithmetic. Music is, in fact, the spoken language of three-dimensional Arithmetic whose measure is also a measure of three: translation, rotations, and reflection. These three transformations are the natural parallels to their biblical counterparts, that of alternation, introversion, and their combination respectively.

Summary List of Biblical Parallels

alpha	numeric	Word
Wisdom	Understanding	Knowledge
Counting	Measuring	Arithmetic
Writing	Arithmetic	Reading
Father	**Holy Spirit**	**God**
Body	**Spirit**	**Soul**
Alternation	Introversion	Chiasm
Psalm	Instrument	Song
(Electricity	Magnetism	Light)

The members in each column are synonymous terms in biblical, parallel thought.

2

All measures in the *Tanakh* are a **these two become one** order of three. Both spiritual and physical measures also parallel one another. Solomon's Model of Instruction parallels the 3R's of modern education.

Knowledge (Reading)

Wisdom (Writing)   *Understanding* (Arithmetic)

According to the Jewish *Midrash*, "intelligence and understanding is greater than wisdom (text) because understanding (number) comes from the mouth of God."[3] The Jewish Sages recorded the following:

> The Jews *saw* the words that came out of the trumpets at Mt. Sinai ... Hebrew letters that flew around the mountain and spoke: *I am God your Lord!*[4]

The Music of *Torah* is HaShem's gift to the soul.[5] What you feed your soul will be judged *measure for measure* on that *Great Day* hailed by the *Last Trumpet Blast*.[6] Two things will cease to exist upon the arrival of The Messiah (according to the Jewish *Talmud*) is idolatry and the music of idolatry. Is it possible, therefore, to extract from Scripture the very rudiments of righteous music dictated from the "mouth" of God? I speak not of <u>words</u>, which is obvious, but the <u>numerical</u> structure of musical

---

[3] Midrash, Ki Sisam 41:3.

[4] Me'Am Lo'Ez, *The Torah Anthology* (Moznaim Publishing Corp., New York, 1990), p. 133.

[5] Spiritual music is, in fact, a reflection of *Torah* structure – a *song*.

[6] The *Last Trumpet Blast* will precede the arrival of The Messiah speaking salvation audibly to the Jews in Hebrew (Exodus 20:15).

compositions and the sound of the instruments – the "word" of an alpha-numeric God.

What we do know from Scripture is that prior to Israel going to war with the nations, the prophets would call upon their instrumental minstrels whose sound communicated audibly with the prophets via the "living" Hebrew alphabet. In fact, music played on instruments alone is considered a Psalm, an instrument of *prophecy*.[7]

The question remains: Did the Lord reveal to King David (the Father of spiritual music) a divine "language" used by the heavenly angels to create righteous, healing music?[8] … Yes, He did, and this study will reveal its secrets and structure. I speak not of the "Higher" Arithmetic taught in public school, nor of biblical ELS codes, gematria, the biblical significance of number, … nor of mathematics, but a holy, Arithmetic language Abraham introduced to the Egyptian mathematicians of sorcery and magic – a language the Egyptians and Greeks were unfamiliar with.[9]

Spiritually speaking, Davidic Music and Abrahamic Arithmetic are one and the same language. Arithmetic is

---

[7] II Kings 3:15. Me'am' Lo'ez, *Tehillim I*, p.41.
[8] Scripture speaks of a divine *Just Balance* (a balance of Rectification and Mercy) AND a *False Balance* – a balance of Judgment. The Jewish Scriptures identify only these two balances.
[9] Josephus, Flavius, *The Complete Works of Josephus*, p.29,33. Jewish tradition, preserved by Josephus, assures us that Adam, Seth, and Enoch introduced Astronomy, not the Chaldeans. Order my book on biblical Arithmetic called ***The Seal of Truth*** (kimthornsburg@yahoo.com).

4

the language the Lord used to structure the Universe, all its laws, forces, vibrations, energy, … and music.[10]

Before we begin this study, I need to introduce you to the biblical language of Arithmetic – the numerical language of <u>understanding</u>. There are many books written on "biblical arithmetic," none of which remotely address the *biblical* "language" called Arithmetic. First and foremost, the Lord communicates only in whole numbers, numbers of finite measures, reciprocity, and symmetry. Man, on the other hand, communicates in symbolic real numbers – numbers of infinite measures, disorder, and chaos.[11]

What is important here is that God identifies <u>two</u> number systems in Scripture – one **good** and righteous, and one **evil** and deceptive. Each number system is assigned a spiritual "balance" and "Identity" (whole or real). These two number balances are also the very templates used to create music – the subject of this study. These balances are not arbitrary inventions of man; on the contrary, <u>they are clearly described</u> in the *Torah* and the *Zohar* – their very number structures and symbols represent the *thoughts* and *ways* of ancient religions.

---

[10] The biblical Law of Correspondence is the template used to create the natural sciences: the Law of Gravity, the Law of Complication III (Chemistry), the Law of Genetics, the order of the DNA Double Helix, the Law of Reciprocity and Harmonics (Mathematics and Music Theory), and the Law of Electromagnetics (Light).

[11] This all is explained in my book *The Seal of Truth* – a corollary to this study. You do not need a math degree to understand biblical Arithmetic – the language of how things are come to be, **the** language of *pure* calculation and *spiritual understanding*!

The Whole Number Balance (WNB) called the *Just Balance* in Scripture

A *these two* [Father and Holy Spirit] *become 1* Pattern of All Things

FATHER

$$\left[\frac{1}{5}, \ \dots \ \frac{1}{3}, \ \frac{1}{2}, \ \mathbf{1}, \ \frac{2}{1}, \ \frac{3}{1}, \ \dots \ \frac{5}{1}\right]$$

←——————— HOLY SPIRIT ———————→

The Real Number Balance (RNB) called the *False Balance* in Scripture[12]

A diverse measure of three separate, unrectified parts

DEATH

$$-\infty \dots \ -3, \ -2, \ -1, \ \mathbf{0}, \ +1, \ +2, \ +3 \ \dots +\infty$$

←——————— HELL ———————→

These balances represent "measures" of good and evil whose music possesses the power to summon heavenly angels or evil spirits. Read the story of King Saul in Scripture. When his musicians played music in his chamber, evil spirits appeared. He threw spears at them in vain; these spirits tortured him constantly. Then, one day a servant informed the King that he knew of a young shepherd boy who played beautiful music on his harp. This young shepherd was David, the son of Jesse.[13]

King Saul summoned David and had him perform on his harp. Immediately the evil spirits fled from the sound of David's harp and legions of angels filled the King's chamber! The sound of David's *kinnor* and the structure of his melodies brought about this miracle and so can instruments and melodies of today.

---

[12] Scripture refers to ZERO (biblical NOTHING) as Death, and INFINITY (biblical VANITY) as Hell. Job 22:4-6; 26:5-7; Isaiah 28:15-18; 34:9-11; **40:15-17**. II Corinthians 7:9-11. Strong's 1077 (*Bal* = biblical *Nothing*).
[13] I Samuel 16:14-23. David is the father of divine, spiritual music.

Keep in mind throughout this study that both the sound of the instrument and the "structure" of the music composition are both scrutinized by the Creator of music. As with the Tree of Life and the Tree of Knowledge of Good and Evil (parallels of the *Just Balance* and the *False Balance* of scripture respectively), these are the **only** spiritual "templates" available to compose music – the Whole Number Balance whose *straight line* of *comely proportion* contains *perfect and just weights;* and the Real Number balance of Mathematic whose *line of confusion* contains *divers stones of emptiness and darkness* - a template whose *false weights* are referred to as *infinite iniquities.*[14] These two balances play a daunting, supernatural role in concealing what is righteous from that which is wicked – none of which is vehemently contested, for the music world of today possess no knowledge of the spiritual language the Lord created to bless his Holy *Name* – that of Whole Number Arithmetic.[15]

Let us begin.

---

[14] Isaiah 34:11; 40:15-17. Abrahamic Arithmetic and Mathematics are two entirely different numerical disciplines … the first came from Heaven above, the latter from the sorcerers of Mystery Babylon. Scripture labels the balance of *comely proportion* as a *Righteous Balance*; whereas, the balance of *infinite iniquities* is referred to as a *Balance of Confusion*. All documented in my book *The Seal of Truth*.
[15] The arithmetic of mathematics is labeled "Higher" Arithmetic in conjunction with "Higher" Mathematics and "Higher" Education professing man's thoughts are "higher" than those of God (Isaiah 55:8,9). To begin with, there is no ZERO (the number of *Baal*) in biblical Arithmetic. The Lord's number is ONE … the Holy ONE.

Music

Speaking to yourselves in psalms and hymns and spiritual songs, singing and making melody in your heart ... For if the trumpet give an __understanding__ sound, who shall prepare himself to the battle?[16]

Biblical music is the "spoken" language of Arithmetic. The sound of the Temple instruments and the sound of the Great Shofar bear witness to the Whole Number Balance (WNB), called the **Pattern of All Things** (PAT) in Scripture. In I Corinthians Chapter 14, the author uses the alpha-numeric motif of *pray-sing*, the "sing" part being that of __understanding__ - a "stringed instrument" (Strong's *5567*). This is an example of biblical, numerical understanding in the form of music. Also note that a *song*, in Hebraic terminology, is a Psalm accompanied with musical instruments. Davidic instruments were considered *instruments of prophecy* whose sound communicated alpha-numerically with the Prophets.

Davidic melodies (biblical *songs*), used in Temple worship, were learned melodies.[17] The musical template was provided to him by God Himself. David's harp (*kinnor*), a "ten-stringed instrument," was emblematic of the Lord's Ten Commandments as were all the musical instruments of the Holy Temple. The Temple Levites **sang**

---

[16] Ephesians 5:19; I Corinthians 14:7, 8, 15. *Pray/sing* ... a __word/number__ motif. When the Trumpets sounded on Mt. Sinai, both words and sound were **seen** and **heard**! _The Torah Anthology_, Exodus III, p.32. Exodus 20:18.

[17] I Chronicles 15:16. Melodies of alternation and introversion.

and *played* on these very Davidic instruments that summoned the *shekinah glory* of God![18]

David awoke every night to the sound of his lyre (*kinnor*) that was hung above his bed. The songs emanating from his harp were performed either by the heavenly angels or God Himself. The Prophet Elisha, through the sound of Davidic instrumental music, called up *the hand of God* to provide the three Kings of Judah, Israel, and Edom a *valley filled with water, that ye may drink, both ye, and your cattle, and your beasts.*[19]

Musical Instruments

According to the Jewish *Midrash*, a psalm is expressed in one of three forms of praise: with recited words (Nitzuah), by musical instruments (Nigun), and by song (Mizmor). A "song"[20] is defined as "chanted Psalms in unison with the playing of instruments."[21] This *Torah* definition is in keeping with the biblical *these two*

---

[18] I Chronicles 15:16; 16:7; 25:3. II Chronicles 5:12-14. As the sons of Jeduthun sang and praised the Lord, David *prophesied with the kinnor (lyre) in thanksgiving.* Hashem placed His prophetic message into the lyre, from which the singer attempted to extract it (Psalm 108:1-3). Musical instruments are channels of prophetic utterances.
[19] II Kings 3:9-17.
[20] According to I Corinthians 14:15, to sing with "spiritual understanding" is to sing with "musical instruments" – a Song. Ephesians 5:17-19 states: *Psalms + Instruments = Spiritual songs.*
[21] Rabbi Shmuel Yerushalmi. *The Torah Anthology: The Book of Tehillim* (Israel: Vagshal Ltd., 1989), p. 41. Strong's 5058, 7892. *5603. The Oxford Companion to Music* (1974, pp.497-499). Psalm 92:1-4.

become one Pattern of All Things and the *Zohar* motif of "word • number = song" – the biblical parallel of Solomon's "wisdom • understanding = knowledge."

It is absolutely paramount to recognize the importance of praising God with appropriate musical instruments, for instrumental music is, in itself, a "Psalm." In reference to Davidic Psalms: "For the Conductor" refers to God who is eternal. "With instrumental music" refers to the **prophetic** faculty, as the scriptures say, *"And it came to pass, when the minstrel played, that the hand of the Lord came upon him."*[22] David was shown the "pattern," in writing and arithmetically, given to Moses on Mt. Sinai – a pattern Solomon used to construct all things associated with the Holy Temple ... including sacred music.

The Hebraic expression **shigayon**, found in many of David's Psalms, refers to "the ecstatic state of the prophet when prophesying."[23] The prayer of Habakkuk the prophet, upon *Shigayon*, speaks of "my instrumental music."[24] According to the Sages, the term "shigayon" identifies a unique poetic form – a *these two become one* form of "alternation and introversion of parts." All things of alternation and introversion are of the King of Glory – HaShem.[25]

---

[22] II Kings 3:15.

[23] Psalm 7:1. *The Torah Anthology: The Book of Trei-Asar (2)*, 1997, pp.190,191.

[24] Habakkuk 3:1,19.

[25] The biblical law of *alternation/introversion* is called the Law of Correspondence. The *Torah* is itself an alternated/introverted Psalm.

The Whole Number Balance is a balance created by alternating and introverting whole number ratios about the unit builder ONE – a balance of reciprocity. The RNB is a balance of opposites whose unit builder is ZERO – a false "whole number" invented by man. There is no ZERO in the Lord's counting and measuring system.[26]

$$[\frac{1}{5}, ... \frac{1}{3}, \frac{1}{2}, \mathbf{1}, \frac{2}{1}, \frac{3}{1}, ... \frac{5}{1}]$$

The whole number balance [1/5,…1/2,**1**,2/1…,5/1] is one of biblical *counting* (1,2,3) and *measuring* (1/3, 1/2, 2/1, 3/1). The whole number ratios (called *stones* or *weights* in Scripture) are bound [having a beginning and an end]. Each ratio is alternated (2 ↔ 2) and introverted (2/1 ↔ 1/2) about the Unit builder ONE. When multiplied together (combined), *these two become ONE* (2/1 • 1/2 = 1, a **rectified** ONE). Pythagoras believed the whole numbers and their unit fractions are sacred and the essence of all creation. Indeed, this Whole Number Balance is the very *Pattern of All Things* (PAT) spoken of throughout the *Tanakh*.

In I Corinthians 14:7-15, we find the <u>numerical aspect</u> of "singing" a Psalm (playing instruments) is that of *spiritual understanding*. The Lord inspired David to write the Psalms and play His melodies on the harp (lyre). The Psalm introduction "For the Conductor; with instrumental music" refers to "chanting the Psalms with instruments" to summon the Holy Spirit.[27]

---

[26] Throughout ancient history, ZERO was/is the number of *Baal* – the god of Chaos – the Egyptian god of Sorcery and Mathematics.
[27] Rabbi Shmuel Yerushalmi. *The Torah Anthology: The Book of Tehillim*, p. 41. Read Psalm 49:4.

Throughout Scripture, God never deviates from integrating the PAT within His music – including the sound of musical instruments (the tuning scale used to perform the music) and the structure of musical melodies or songs. Not all music, however, gives glory to the Lord.

There are other forms of music void of biblical harmony and understanding (including the types of instruments used and their tuning frequencies). If structure and sound are not according the Lord's *Pattern of All Things* (PAT), the music will, will indeed, summon evil spirits.

> *Take thou away from me the noise of thy songs [tuning frequencies]; for I will not hear [understand] the melody of thy viols ... That chant to the sound of the viol, and invent to themselves instruments of music, like David.*[28]   *(Amos 5:23; 6:5)*

We are about to delve into the spiritual realm of biblical understanding that need be rediscovered. Is there another musical balance or "template" used by the musicians of *Baal* and the sorcerers (priests) of Mystery Babylon? Indeed, there is, and it is well documented in the *Torah*, in the *Zohar*, and reiterated in the Book of Enoch.

> *Then a herald proclaimed in a loud voice, to you it is commanded, O people, nations, and languages, that at what time ye hear the sound of the horn, pipe, zither, lyre, psaltery, and all types of instruments [non-harmonic fequencies], ye fall down and worship the statue of gold that Nebuchadnezzar the king [of Babylon] hath set up.*

---

[28] Daniel 3:5. The words *melody* and *noise* refer to the composition *structure* and the tuning *frequency* used to perform their songs.

A good Bible concordance will inform you that the music of Dura[29] "memorized, placed in a trance" the worshippers of *Baal* with the exception of Daniel's three friends Shadrach, Meshach, and Abednego. In this story, not only was the **sound** (frequency) of the instruments enchanting, the **structure** of the music was also of primary significance. Perhaps we ought to investigate the tuning methods of Babylonian music, adopted by the Egyptian and Greek magicians - in particular, the music of the "sacred mysteries" derived, in part, from the "sacred" priests of Mystery Babylon ... the Anaki.

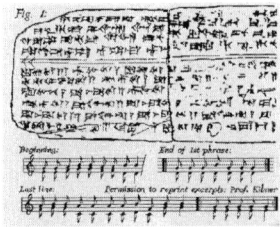

The earliest account of the Anunnaki (Nephilim Giants) can be found on Sumerian tablets. For ancient Sumerians, music was the tool that helped them to describe the universe.[30]

The Sound of *Baal*

The music of ancient Mesopotamia, India, Greece, and Egypt was/is based on a "spiral of fifths" scale, slightly different from the "circle of fifths" scale of modern Western music. The ancient spiral of fifths tuning would

---

[29] Daniel 3:1-5. Daniel uses the *voice • speech = Song* motif of the *Torah* and *Zohar*; however, "speech" may include *all types of non-kosher instruments* referring to the sound of the *Malkhut of the Other Side* – instruments tuned to Pythagorean ratios and 432hz.

[30] *The Shining Ones from Ancient Mesopotamia*, Freedomtek.org

eventually become known as "Pythagorean Tuning." The Greek Eleusinica Mysteries, Egyptian mysteries, as well as Phoenicians and Shamans of archaic Mesopotamians used Pythagorean tuning to "induce their shamanic ecstasies and oracular union with the stellar gods – the Anaki."[31] The Sumerians acquired Pythagorean tuning and 432hz from the "Shining Ones." Sumerian tablets from a library in Nippur identify these Shining Ones as the "Anunnaki."[32]

The Shining Ones

According to Enoch, Noah, Abraham and the Jewish Sages, "the *Anakim* [giants] were the offspring of the illicit union of the descended angels [Nephilim] on Mount Hermon and the daughters of Cain ... They were so called because they fell and caused the world to fall (Rashi) ... and they filled the world with abortions through their immorality."[33] According to the Talmud, the Nephilim giant *Og* survived the Flood and possibly other giants as noted by the Sumerian tablets in Nippur and elsewhere in Scripture.[34] Not only is Mt. Hermon the sight where the Nephilim (angelic offspring) fell from Heaven, they are credited with the origin of *Baal* worship (the first Trinitarian religion), sorcery, and Pythagorean Tuning.

---

[31] The Net: *The Earth Changes Central & American AntiFedrealist Forums.* This is a good site to study the lore of Sacred Geometry. Pythagorean tuning is a metaphor for "snake or dragon eating its own tail" called "serpent tuning." Greek modes descended from Assyrian lyre tunings of the second millennium B.C. and tuned (by inference) to the spiral of fifths ratios [Pythagorean tuning] preferred in Greece. *Sounds from Silence: Recent Discoveries in Ancient Near Eastern Music* (Berkeley: Bit Enki Publications, 1976).

[32] Freedomtek.org. *Fallen Angels, Anunnaki, Nephilim, Watchers – The Shining Ones from Ancient Mesopotamia.* McCain, Ernest. Epigraphical Society Occasional Papers, 2001, *The forgotten harmonical science of the Bible*, p.8.

[33] *ArtSchroll Tanakh Series*, Genesis Vol. 1 (Mesorah Publications, Ltd., Brooklyn, N.Y., 1977), pp.186, 187.

[34] Read *The Books of Enoch* (Fifth Estate, 2009), p. 213.

What do Heavy Metal and Hard Rock bands have in common with the Babylonian musicians and instruments of Dura? They also tune their instruments to Pythagorean and Just Intonation ratios to enchant their listeners! [35] Their ritual tuning systems are employed by Hindu priests, Tibetan monks, new age and occult gurus, Theoretical Kabbalists, astrologers, Satanists, and the keepers of the sacred mysteries (Sacred Geometry) of Babylon – tuning sacred to *Baal*, but not to HaShem.

Pop messiahs of the age ushered in the return of the Beast.[36] Satanist Aleister Crowley appears on Peter Blake's cover of the Beatles' Sgt. Pepper's Lonely Hearts

---

[35] "Everything Plato and Aristotle learned about mathematics they learned from Pythagoras. His Pythagorean Brotherhood had an effect on future esoteric traditions, such as Freemasonry and Rosicrucianism, both of which were scientific/mystical groups dedicated to the study of Mathematics and Sacred Geometry." Hall, Manly. *The Secret Teachings of All Ages,* chapter entitled "Pythagorean Mathematics." (Aristotle rebuked the wisdom of Pythagoras!)

[36] *Heavy Metal Times*, May 1983. Jimi Hendrix "believed he was possessed by some spirit and did not have control of it." Jim Morrison (The Doors) called the spirits that possessed him "the Lords." Led Zeppelin's Jimmy Page, a self-confessed Satanist, bought Aleister Crowley's old mansion (who also glorified 432hz and Pythagorean tuning). Members of the group Iron Maiden openly admit that they are dabbling in the occult, including witchcraft. Peter Criss (Kiss), Glenn Tipton (Judas Priest), Stevie Nicks (Fleetwood Mac), Ozzy Osbourne (Black Sabbath), John Lennon (The Beatles) all profess to have had involvement with spirit guides, automatic writing, the occult, and *Baal* worship. Crackmagazine.net. Quote from *Turn and Face The Strange – Occultist Aleister Crowley's Influence of Popular Music* by Louder than War (internet).

Club Band. A statue of Crowley also appears on the cover of the Doors' album, Doors 13. Mick Jagger was seen carrying occult books ahead of the Stones album "His Satanic Majesties," that cradled one of their most anthemic songs; "Sympathy for the Devil."

> I was directed and commanded by another power ... The power of darkness ... the power of the devil."
>
> Little Richard

> "Rock has always been devil's music." David Bowie

> "Demonic, that's what we are." Mic Mars (Motley Crue)

> "I'm going to abandon my spirit to them ... and fall in supplication of the demon gods." David Roth (Van Halen)

Western instruments of today are tuned using an equal-tempered "circle of fifths" scale (all 12 notes of the scale are of equal spacing). The music of the *Anaki* and the instruments of *Baal* (biblical "plain of Dura"), however, were tuned using a Pythagorean "spiral of fifths" (a non-harmonic scale of unequal spacing). Furthermore, the Anaki-Pythagorean tuning <u>required</u> the fundamental frequency to be tuned to a specific frequency (432 Hz) - **a frequency sacred to pagan rituals, Sun-pyramids, and temples dedicated to the Trinitarian Sun-god *Baal*.**[37]

---

[37] It is said that Hitler, a truly possessed soul, purposed to change the dominate pitch of music from 432hz to 440hz, thus suggesting 440hz is an anathema to "good" music. Of course, these individuals conveniently ignore the fact that Hitler capitulated to an International Conference held in 1939 in which the nations of the

It is the structure and tuning of unholy compositions the Lord finds detestable. The sound of the instruments used in the Holy Temple as well as the structure of the Davidic compositions, however, were ordained by the Hand of God according to His "Pattern of All Things."

Melody and Noise of Baal

The *Torah* and the prophets have much to say about the music of the Nephilim (Anaki) who introduced *Baal* worship to the Sumerians (Chaldeans/Babylonians), Egypt, and Greece. The following is a list of passages in the *Tanakh* related directly to the "sound" and "melody" of *Baal* music.

> Spare Me the sound of your hymns, and let Me not hear the music of your lutes … They hum snatches of song to the tune of the lute accounting themselves musicians like David.
> Amos 5:23; 6:5

Moloch and Chiun are among the gods of *Baal* worship. It is important to note here in Amos 5:23 that the *sound of your hymns* is in reference to the frequencies or tuning used to perform the music. The expression *hum snatches of song to the tune of the lute* is in reference to the compositional <u>structure</u> of a *song* (or hymn) … they did not use the pattern of all things to compose their songs.

---

world agreed to adopt A=440 as the standard pitch. Germany produced some of the greatest symphonic, 440hz composers using the equal-temperament tuning, not Pythagorean tuning.

The wicked *account themselves musicians like David* (6:5) – they invent and alter the vibrational frequencies of their instruments.[38] The Lord here in the Book of Amos is speaking of the music of *Baal* - the Trinity *SUN-god* of Babylonia, Egypt, Greece, and India.[39]

HaShem was sure to address the effect of music the wicked listen to, and when listening to the music of HaShem, they failed to understand the significance of the songs (melody, harmony, and reciprocity). So too today musicians fail to understand the significance of equal-temperament tuning AND **the arithmetic construct of their songs, in particular, the *pattern of all things*.**

> *To them you are just a singer of bawdy songs, who has a sweet voice and plays skillfully; they hear your words [of prophecy] but will not obey them.*[40] *But when it comes – and come it will – they shall know that a prophet has been among them.*   *(Ezekiel 33:30-32)*

---

[38] The electric guitar and the electric piano cannot produce natural harmonic frequencies. These instruments are designed to play music with varying intonations and unconventional chords.

[39] The archaic Egyptian and Babylonian instruments that have been unearthed by archeologists and those of ancient Greece were predominately tuned to 432Hz. Greek spiral of fifths ratios (Pythagorean tuning) descended from Assyrian lyre tunings of the second millennium B.C. Kilmer, Crocker and Brown. *Sounds from Silence: Recent Discoveries in Ancient Near Eastern Music*, 1976.

[40] They hear the *sound,* but only the soul can hear the *words* of prophetic music. Davidic music is prophetic music! All the nations saw and heard the *sound* of the Lord's Trumpets on Mt. Sinai but only the Jews saw the prophetic *words* that came forth from the Trumpets and spoke to them: "I am the God of Israel."

The prophet Ezekiel addresses 7 things on the day of judgment that will *come to an end*, two of which are *the murmur of your songs*[41] and the *sound of your lyres.*[42]

Rock Music

The Spirit of Rock music is the same Spirit that led Israel into *Baal* worship. Let us compare the time of Ezra, when Israel turned from HaShem seeking the comfort of false prophets and *Baal*, with that of the 1960's "Hippy" movement and the introduction of "Rock" music and rebellion. Contrast the temperament of a symphonic audience with that of most rock audiences.

EZRA	1960
The wicked invented new instruments to worship Baal. The Lord called the sound of these instruments "noise" — the *noise of rebellion,* for these instruments **could not produce natural harmonic tones**.	Those that introduced the Rock culture invented instruments (electrical) that cannot produce "natural" harmonic tones. Many of the Rock stars were/are actively involved with the occult and Satanism.
Baal worship involved all aspects of self-worship, tattoos, demonic amulets, and sexual perversions, that lead to all types of spiritual abominations, sorcery and demonic symbolism.	The Rock culture engage in all types of sexual perversions, tattoos, the wearing of occultic amulets (the cross, Egyptian Ankh, all-seeing eye, peace symbol, and the yin-yang), and embrace abortions.
No fear of God. No modesty.	No fear of God. No modesty.
They call evil good and good evil.	They call evil good and good evil.

---

[41] The "structure" and sound of Anaki music does not adhere to the arithmetic Pattern of All Things. "Sound" refers to the tuning frequencies used – mathematical or arithmetic frequencies.
[42] Ezekiel 26:13-17.

According to the *Torah*, altering the structure of music alters the melody of spiritual (Davidic) music. The three friends of Daniel ("Plain of Dura," 3:10-30) knew this and were immune to the <u>music</u> and <u>sound</u> of the Anaki. In II Chronicles 5:12-14 and 7:1-3, the music of David *drew down the fire of Heaven, and the glory of the Lord upon the house, they bowed themselves with their faces to the ground and worshipped and praised the Father in Heaven.* <u>Your spiritual understanding is contingent upon the music you listen to</u>. All is *measure for measure.*

The Music of Torah

The Jewish historian Philo of Alexandria concluded that the Hebrew prophet Moses must have understood tuning theory long before Pythagoras brought it home to Greece. Commenting on *Genesis* early in the first century AD, Philo recognized that tribal narrative carries symbolic meaning in harmonic theory.[43] Gleaning from the works of Philo, music Professor Ernest McCain came to the unwavering conclusion that the *Torah* "brilliantly allegorizes every aspect of Diophantine approximation to modern Equal-Temperament."[44]

---

[43] *The Forgotten harmonical science of the Bible*, Ernest B. McCain. In other words, "<u>Philo believed the template for writing the *Torah* was identical to the fundamental rudiments of music theory</u>" ... and it is! The written text of the *Torah* is structured via alternation and introversion – a mere image of the pattern of all things (the WNB), invoking the very laws of whole number arithmetic.

[44] In number theory, the field of Diophantine approximation, named after Diophantus of Alexandria, deals with the approximation of real

McCain explains the basics of tuning theory and the graphic use of the monochord string tuned into a 'tonal circle' on which any scale can be represented geometrically. McCain refers to this "tonal circle" as an equal- temperament scale constructed using the circle of fifths. He further suggests that this equal-temperament scale may have been known as far back as the 3rd millennium BC in ancient Samaria.

> McCain made an intellectual breakthrough of the utmost significance by offering a simple musical explanation of crucial passages of texts of world literature (the Rg Veda, the Egyptian Book of the Dead, the Bible, Plato) that have defied critics of the separate concerned disciplines ... taking numbers from monochord tuning, McCain identified their widespread employment in numerical allegories, myths, and metaphors found in some of the oldest books in the world. McCain decoded many musical allegories and discovered the meaning of some incredibly large numbers in Babylonian, Egyptian, Hindu, Greek, and Hebrew texts ... In his book _The Pythagorean Plato_ [1978].[45]

If Philo's understanding of tribal mythology and music is indeed founded upon sound logic, then is it possible that the Temple music of the Jewish nation was based on equal-temperament, whole number ratios? Biblical,

---

numbers by rational whole numbers. Ernest G. McCain, professor emeritus of music at Brooklyn College, is known for his efforts to establish the ancient mathematical discipline of music as the means to unlock the deepest meaning of history's great religious and philosophical texts. The Lord's Pattern of All Things uses exact whole number ratios and frequencies, nothing is approximated with God.
[45] Graham Pont. _Nexus Network Journal._

whole number ratios also play a key role in composing Davidic music – music that glorifies the Creator.[46]

"The equal responsibilities assigned to 12 tribes of radically different sizes points toward 12-tone equal division as an idealist norm ... I treat Davidic tunings as approximations to equal-temperament and try to ignore everything but the recovery of authorial tonal models. Only the Bible's own *arithmetic* and its own statements about it can be trusted. No later commentator has ever equaled Philo's insight. Although his own arithmetic often proves inadequate, his clues remain priceless ... **Bible [Jewish] authors were far more expert with this matrix arithmetic than any later scholars have proved to be ... forgotten tonal logic (Abrahamic Arithmetic) is biblical numerology, employed with perfect discipline by Bible authors from the First page of *Genesis* to Last page of *Revelation*.**"[47]

What we do know about Davidic Temple music is that the ritual ceremonies, Temple and furniture measurements, and all things related to Temple worship (including music) were commanded by God to be in accordance with biblical arithmetic. Unlike the instrumental melodies of Dura and that of the mixed multitude who produced the Golden Calf (both of Pythagorean tuning), the harmonic melodies of David were constructed according to a divinely inspired, whole number "template" whose sound banished demonic spirits from his presence and summoned the *shekinah* glory of God![48]

---

[46] I Corinthians Chapter 14 and the *Tanakh* correlates "sing" to a *musical string* and arithmetic understanding (McCain's Monochord) of reciprocity (not that of the Pythagorean, irrational ratios). Strong's *2433, 356-303, 5567*.

[47] *The forgotten harmonical science of the Bible*, pp. 3,4.

[48] 1 Samuel 16:23; II Chronicles 5:12-14. *The Torah Anthology*: Book of *Samuel 1*, (Moznaim Publishing, 1991), p. 250.

The Books of Ezekiel and Revelation have something to say about the New Jerusalem and the Tree of Life – a unique metaphor for heavenly music. Concerning the New Jerusalem and the river of life that flows within its veins, scripture informs us that the Tree of Life in the midst of the river *bares twelve manner of fruit* (12 chromatic tones), *yielding her fruit every month* (12 equal intervals of 30 days – lunar calendar), *and the leaves of the tree* (the 12 tribes of Israel) *are for the healing of the nations who kept the commandment of God* - a perfect description of equal-tempered music whose biblical *measure* of the Tree of Life is three (12,12,12).[49]

> Concerning the equal-temperament circle of fifths, if the fundamental [note] is assigned a relative frequency of 1 unit then proceeding clockwise around the tone circle one arrives at the identical tone one octave higher with a relative frequency of 2. A revolution in the counterclockwise direction results in a 481 tone one octave lower at a relative frequency of ½. It is the **miracle** of music that if the ratio of frequencies of two tones is a multiple of 2, the tones are perceived by the ear to be identical.[50] As a result, each tone will be considered a member of a pitch class of tones differing

---

[49] A **"voice • speech = Song"** *Zohar* motif. Psalms 1:3-6; Ezekiel 47:12,13; Revelation 22:1-3. "Music, Healing and Longevity" by Mao Shing Ni, D.O.M., PhD. It has been shown scientifically that the "sound" of symphonic music can and does heal the body and adds years to a person's life. This applies to plant life and production. Dr. T.C. Singh. Botany Department of Annamalia University, India, 1962.

[50] The "double octave" (a *these two become one **miracle***) is the basic unit of the Bible. McClain refers to this mode as being the "menorah model" since it refers to the seven-branched candlestick in Exodus 25:31-40 and found today in all synagogues. Notice that this "double octave" frequency of equal-temperament is a *these two become one, times (2),time (1),half-time(½)* prophetic utterance.

in frequency by a multiple of 2. The chromatic scale equally divides the tone circle and as a result is referred to as an equal-tempered scale. The norm in the Torah is to use a double octave, i.e., 1:2::2:4, which also corresponds to Hebrews gematria for "Eden," 124, ... Hebrew letters also have numerical values.[51]

Let's get back to McCain's original research that included both the Equal-Temperament and Pythagorean tuning systems – both of which are referred metaphorically in Scripture. His own research led McCain to associate "Davidic music" to the equal-tempered system; whereas the Pythagorean tuning system was used exclusively by the Babylonian, Egyptian and Greek (Hindu and Buddhist priests included) mystery religions of *Baal* – religions associated with the Anaki and biblical "giants."

The Sound of Equal-Tempered Music
of
Alternation and Introversion

The structure of equal-temperament music is built around chords consisting of the fundamental, major 3rd and 5th [alternated] known as the major triad and the fundamental, minor 3rd and 5th [introverted intervals of DNA], the minor triad. The unison (1:1 ratio), octave, 4th, 5th [reciprocals of one another], major and minor 3rds, and major and minor 6ths are the only consonant intervals of the chromatic scale.

Both the structure of a Davidic composition and the tuning frequencies must adhere to biblical alternation, introversion, and the combination of both (called a *chiasm*). Most of the secular, non-symphonic music of today does not conform to this Pattern of All Things.

---

[51] Kappraff, Jay. *The Lost Harmonic Law of the Bible*, New Jersey Institute of Technology, Newark, NJ.

Adopting a fundamental frequency of 432hz or any other frequency does not produce Pythagorean intervals. It is the frequency **scale** (Equal, Just Intonation, or Pythagorean intervals) the composer chooses to create harmonic or non-harmonic music. According to the Anaki, however, the composer MUST adopt 432hz for the tonic frequency, combined with Pythagorean/Just Intonation ratios (ratios of infinite measures derived from mathematics) that induce the sound of *sorcery.*[52]

According to McCain, the Pythagorean ratios (metaphorically) are exemplified in Greek mythology giving "rise to a wealth of sexual imagery in the Rg Veda in which this region is pictured as a 'vagina' while the wedge to the center of the circle is a *sepah* or 'penis.' The whole construction arises from an interplay of 'male' and 'female' in which the musical commas (unnatural frequencies) that arise are a kind of genital friction."[53] This religious symbolism is reiterated not only in Greek, Egyptian, Indian mythology, it is the core essence of their Sacred Geometry.

> Torah arithmetic is based on the numbers 1,2,3,4,5,6,7. In Genesis the first six days are used for the work of constructing the world while the seventh day is reserved for God. To construct tunings using musical fifths, only the numbers 1,2,3,4 and 6 were used, but the chromatic scale requires six-digit numbers. There are also references in the Bible to the "Anakim" or "giants" from whom the

---

[52] Exodus 32:17,18. We know the music of the Golden Calf was created by the Anakim (the biblical *mixed multitude*) via sorcery.
[53] Kappraff. p.484. Pythagorean ratios, in music terminology, are synonymous with Greek "vagina/penis" motifs of *Baal* worship.

Chosen win the "Holy Land" (Deut. 1:28) with another tuning [equal-temperament] represented by smaller numbers. These Anakim correspond to the huge numbers (∞) and slightly excessive spiral of fifths. In Greek mythology, 5 is the number assigned to humans." This number will reduce the numerosity of the chromatic scale from six digits to a mere two or three digits.[54]

This information is presented here to enlighten the reader to the fact that Scripture does, indeed, identify two systems of spiritual logic – the *straight path* (reciprocal, harmonic symmetries) and the *crooked path* (asymmetrical, non-harmonic opposites). Not only does this include the **numbers** of God as opposed to those of man, but also the **melody** of the whole number music as opposed to the faint sound of real number music (non-harmonic noise that does not employ alternation and introversion ratios).

Is it any wonder that the proponents of Pythagorean/Just intonation tuning are not amicable with the sound of equal-temperament tuning? Also, it is not surprising the Fathers of Higher Mathematics declare their numerical logic "Higher" than that of He who created the universe? Notice also that the structure of the Anaki's Pythagorean tuning (p. 30) employs three distinct divisions (a Trinity).

Goldschmidt Series

A most important discovery on the periodic structure of chemical elements by geochemist Victor Goldschmidt quite literally supports, if not confirms, McCain's

---

[54] Ibid. p. 485. Natural sciences are of alternation and introversion.

supposition that there exists an invariant, universal tonal scale of which "any scale (of natural frequencies) can be represented geometrically."[55] Using the Victor Goldschmidt "complication model," if one were to transform arithmetically the frequencies of light and sound about the dominate color of the rainbow or fundamental note of an equal-tempered scale, the natural harmonic progression of frequencies would follow:

Natural String Vibration
(string length)   (vibration)
1/2, 2/3, 3/4, 1, 4/3, 3/2, 2

Goldschmidt Chord Series

0   1/3   .   .   1   .   .   .   ∞
Major Common Chord (Root Position)
0   1/3   .   .   1   .   2   .   ∞
Minor Common Chord (First Inversion)
0   .   1/2 .   1   .   2   .   ∞
Major Common Chord (Second Inversion)
0   1/3   .   .   1   .   .   3   ∞
Chord of the Dominant Seventh

Goldschmidt Color Series

0	1/3	1/2	.	1	.	2	3	∞
Purple	Scarlet	Red		Yellow		Green	Blue	Violet

Goldschmidt Major Planets Distance from Sun

0	.	1/2	.	1	.	2	3	∞
Sun		Jupiter		Saturn		Uranus	Neptune	Space

---

[55] M. A. Peacock, New Haven, Connecticut. *CALAVERITE AND THE LAW OF COMPLICATION.*

"This unity of sound and light by mathematical formula produces a single, rational whole number series of universal order **harmonious to all natural phenomena** … the deep significance of this law cannot be doubted, albeit its physical basis is even now vaguely outlined …" The truth of the matter is that any naturally occurring series of frequencies in nature can be transformed into a Goldschmidt normal scale of **alternating and introverted whole number ratios** precisely as Professor McCain and Philo of Alexandria (and Johannes Kepler) had suggested.

Professor Goldschmidt found that the majority of crystal structures could be categorized with no higher order that complication level III.[56] No crystalline structure is more complicated than one of three identifiable arrangements of faces and angle measurements.[57] The principal "nodes" in the Goldschmidt series are analogous to the Fraunhofer endpoints of the solar spectrum and the *octave* of the equal-temperament balance.

Music, according to the Jewish Sages, is the most elevated hallmark of the entire universe. The 7 notes of the ancient Jewish music scale are patterned after 7 planets that are in our solar system that encompass the

---

[56] This law corresponds with "Rashi's Formula" of alternation and introversion (Exodus 14:19-21) concerning the structure of all the Names of God **AND** the 3-dimensional structure of crystals.

[57] Crystalline structures are composed of only three transformational operations − that of translations, rotations, and reflections … synonymous with biblical alternations, introversions, and their combination (*chiasms*) − the pattern of all scientific phenomena.

Earth. As Goldschmidt has shown, the distances from the Sun to each of these 7 planets corresponds precisely with the <u>Geometric Mean</u> of the arithmetic balance … not the Pythagorean <u>Golden Proportion</u> (Φ) and its false "Music of the Spheres."

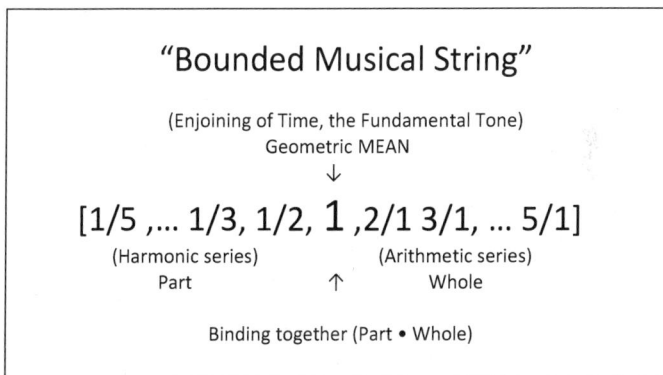

"Bounded Musical String"

(Enjoining of Time, the Fundamental Tone)
Geometric MEAN
↓

$$[1/5 ,… 1/3, 1/2, 1 ,2/1\ 3/1, … 5/1]$$

(Harmonic series)		(Arithmetic series)
Part	↑	Whole

Binding together (Part • Whole)

All things of Creation mirror this unique musical pattern of alternation and introversion. What is significant about this observation is that the *Torah* itself is structured after this very arithmetic pattern of reciprocity. Equal-tempered tuning is the true tuning of the Cosmos, not the pagan, Anaki-Pythagorean tuning, for its ratios do not conform to true Universal harmony.

One final observation concerning the pattern of Anaki-Pythagorean intervals, peculiar only to the selection of 432Hz as the fundamental frequency … the resulting differences between "circle of fifths" and "spiral of fifths" intervals produce a most profound balance.

... -5.87, -3.91, -1.96, **0**, +1.96, +3.91, +5.87 ...

If we select 1.96 as an imaginary 1, then 3.91 = 2, then 5.87 = 3 and so forth, the resulting balance created from these *infinite quantities* would transform into:

... -3, -2, -1, **0**, +1, +2, +3 ...

The Real Number Balance of sorcery and Higher Mathematics.

Biblical Reckoning

Both the <u>spiral of fifths</u> and <u>circle of fifths</u> scales are diatonic scales exhibiting a harmonic sequence of whole and half steps. The Pythagorean and Just Intonation scales, cyclic systems constructed with "pure" intervals, becomes more and more dissonant in sound as we ascend its chromatic intervals, creating what is referred to as "noise" or Pythagorean comma. This is a result of the differences in ascending chromatic tones. The equal-temperament scale of 12 equal-sized semitones, however, enabled instruments to play in all keys of the chromatic system with minimal flaws in intonation.

It is also interesting to note that within the equal-temperament, heptatonic-diatonic tonal-system, only the octave (*eighth interval*) is acoustically *pure*. Unlike Pythagorean and Just intonation, the eighth interval in equal-temperament remains "pure" throughout the chromatic keys. So too do we find 7 days of prayer and fasting throughout the Lord's festival seasons culminate in an *eighty-day* – a holy *"pure"* convocation of rest. The eight-day (Shemini Atzeret) of the Feast of Tabernacles is identified by the Lord Himself as *"The Last Great Day"* – the Sabbath of redemption.

Notice that the "pure," *eighth* interval in the equal-temperament system is separated from the preceding seven notes as also are the preceding seven days of Shemini Atzeret - the *Eighth-day* of the feast of Sukkot.[58] Also, on the *eighth* day are all Jewish born males to be circumcised as a "sign" that they are the chosen among all the nations of the world and points to a future day of perfection and redemption – the perfect *eight* interval or the "perfect" *Eight Day* of Shemini Atzerat.[59]

Musical Chiasms

Chiastic "musical" structures in Scripture are an excellent example of how the Lord communicates the Pattern of All Things alpha-numerically throughout the universe. These structures also provide imminent support for Ernest McCain's methodology of decoding Scripture, for biblical chiastic structures provide a literal presentation of biblical, alpha-numeric parallels ... all structured after a *these two become one* biblical pattern of alternation/introversion - called the **Seal of Truth**.[60]

---

[58] Leviticus 23:34-36. The *gematria* of 8 is "a new beginning."

[59] Beware of those who teach "replacement theology." The Lord's Festivals follow an equal-temperament time-frame whose 8th Day or "perfect" octave points to *Israel's* day of adoption and redemption!

[60] The combined structures of the Hebrew letters *Alef* and *Tav* make up the structure of the WNB (PAT) from whence it received its name *The Seal of Truth*. Rabbi Aaron Raskin, *Letters of Light* (Third Edition) pp. 221-3.

Bach, Chopin, Beethoven, Schubert, List, Schumann, Brahms, Mozart, Hayden and the great composers of the Baroque, Classical and Romantic eras were all well acquainted with the spiritual significance of music. Johann Sebastian Bach composed voice and instrument *chiastic* structures in his music that parallel chiastic structures found in Scripture. A "chiastic" (text or instrumental) structure incorporates a combination motif of alternations and introversions – the tonal aspect of a *comely proportion* (reciprocity). Chiastic, alpha-numeric structures are rarely employed in secular music.

> This chapter [I Chronicles 25] is the true foundation for all God-pleasing music ... splendid proof that music was instituted by the Spirit of God through David.[61]

The relationship between alternating and introversion of parts, in arithmetic vernacular, is called "reciprocity." Thus, according to the Word of God, "voice" and "instruments" (the *kinnor* in particular) are **reciprocal** components of their combined whole (a SONG)[62] – as are all the reciprocal parts of the whole number balance (i.e. $1/2 \cdot 2/1 = 1$). A Davidic parallel to Bach's chiastic songs can be found in II Chronicles 5:12-14.

$$\text{Voice} \quad \bullet \quad \text{Instruments} \quad = \quad \text{One}$$

Voice	Instruments	One
(Singers)	(Trumpets)	(Song)

---

[61] Notes found in Bach's biblical commentary. Patrick Kavannaugh. *The Spiritual Lives of Great Composers* (Sparrow Press,1992), p.15.
[62] "Speech (or musical instruments) rectifies Voice via multiplication." From *Zohar* teaching. Rebbe Nachmann, _Likutey Moharan_ (Breslov Research Institute, Jerusalem, 2012), p. 96.

According to Solomon, wisdom (writing, text) and understanding (counting and measuring) complement each other, they work together in unison *adding life to all those who study the Torah* (knowledge).[63] The power of this alpha-numeric "union" is that of multiplication [reciprocity] as is the power of the WNB. All alpha-numeric motifs in Scripture are a *these two become one* motif by the *power* of multiplication.[64] The following Psalm is an excellent parallel of an **alpha** "writing/counting" **numeric** "singer/instrument" chiastic structure found in Scripture.

> The Lord shall count [number], when he writteth [text or name] up the people, that this man was born there ... As well the **singers** [text] as the **players** on instruments [number] shall be there: all my springs are in thee.   (Psalm 87:6,7)

Biblical Chiasms

"The alternation and introversion structures of the Holy Bible "give, not a mere Analysis evolved from the Text by human ingenuity, but a Symmetrical Exhibition of the Word itself, which may be discerned by the humblest reader of the Sacred Text and seen to be one of the most important evidences of the Divine Inspiration of its words. For these Structures constitute a remarkable phenomenon peculiar to Divine Revelation; and are not found outside it in any other form of known literature."[65]

Hebraic parallelism is the process of alternating and introverting an idea in diverse ways. Not only do we find simple and complex structures throughout Scripture, the

---

[63] Psalms 3 and 4:1-10; Jeremiah 3:15-16. The Jewish *Shema* includes *Eloheniu* (counting) and *Echad* (measuring) ... arithmetic 1 and WNB.

[64] The *power* of the RNB is division.

[65] *The Companion Bible*, Kregel Publications, by Dr. E.W. Bullinger. The entire Companion Bible is formatted with chiastic structures.

world as we understand it is a unique whole number structure as well. There are those who suggest the Book of Esther is a chiastic structure, when, in fact, the entire Word of God is written in chiastic structures. Take, for example, the chiastic structure of Psalm 119.

Prayer. Teaching.
(Introversion and Alternation)
A chiastic text numerically structured according to the WNB

X | t | 33. Eyes. Make me to see.
   | u | 34-. Mind. Its comprehension.
     Y | -34. Heart.
       Z | 35. Feet. Practical walking.
     Y | 36. Heart.
X | t | 37-39. Eyes. Turn them away.
   | u | 40. Mind. Its desires.

Here within this structure, we find the use of alternating (X↔X; t/u↔ t/u) and introversion (X, Y, Z, Y, X) of parts – the center of introversion being the letter Z. Parallel structures simply restate an idea with "parallel" phrases and words. The alternated structure found in Psalm 119:105 is a good example to clarify this process.

Your word is a lamp to my feet and a light to my path.

The expressions "lamp to my feet" and "light to my path" are alternated (repeated) parallel thoughts. Also, the words "lamp↔light" and "feet↔path" are paralleled.

The Power of Song

The Jewish Sages taught that when a miracle occurs for a person and he/she *sings to God in thanksgiving*, they are guaranteed that all their sins are forgiven.[66] Consider the Song of Moses when God miraculously redeemed Israel from the Egyptian army through the Red Sea. The Song of Moses, found in Exodus 15:1-17, was written with a special, chiastic "pattern" – a derivation of the PAT. If copied incorrectly, the scroll becomes invalid.[67]

The youth of today, having succumb to the venomous songs of the Anaki, wholeheartedly embrace the spirit of rebellion and loathe the sound of prophecy and understanding (symphonic and chiastic music). Taking God out of our schools is not the only issue here, it is also the music they listen to. One aspect of the judgment of the wicked is the music they listen to (what they feed their soul).[68] Consider the thoughts of one schooled in mathematics[69] and secular music whose thoughts are those of man - secular thoughts void of scientific and spiritual understanding:

---

[66] Me'Am Lo'Ez. *The Torah Anthology*, p. 245., Psalms 18:1.

[67] Ibid. pp. 242,243.

[68] There are many professors of music and composers today that berate equal-temperament tuning. Many of these intellectuals also embrace 432hz as the preferred tonal frequency. They masterfully craft bold assumptions based on their own preferences - anything to malign the works of our Creator as do mathematicians whose Calculus embraces the very symbolism of hieroglyphic *Baal* worship including 432, the Real Number Scale, the Golden Ratio, ZERO and INFINITE chaos – what the prophet Isaiah *counted as nothing, less than nothing; One who chooses you is an abomination (41:23,24).*

[69] The *Zohar* reveals the very numerical structure of the Balance of Judgment – **an exact copy of the Real Number *Scale* of Modern Mathematics and Pythagorean tuning.** *Zohar*, Beresheet A, p. 180.

The music of today does not limit the concept of symmetry to a sense of a good [comely] proportion and a symmetrical, well-balanced concordance [alternation/introversion] of parts. The art of movements in the last seventy years has brought into question all the traditional aesthetic rules, so we can no longer say: "Beauty is bound up with symmetry." The established rules no longer dictate what constitutes beauty ... asymmetry [Pythagorean/Just intonation, chaos] makes headway towards a *new* symmetrical order.[70]

As the Lord stated, man's ways are not His ways and man's thoughts[71] are not those of God nor does secular music glorify the *Name* of God. The *sound* of the *kinnor* communicated (audibly) with the soul of David as it did with Solomon, Elisha, and the rest of the Prophets of God. So too does the Spirit of *Baal* and the non-chiastic, asymmetrical structures of the Anakim communicate with the soul of the rebellious.[72]

When Moses came down from Mt. Sinai with the Ten Commandments, God spoke to him telling Moses that He (God) could hear the "sound of rebellion" coming forth

---

[70] The very thoughts of New Age Occultist Benjamin Crème: "A New Religion (including Freemasonry) will manifest the occult mysteries, wrapped up on number, metaphor, and symbol." *Symmetry: Unifying Human Understanding*, International Series in Mathematics and Computer Science (Pergamon Press), p. 436.

[71] *"Thoughts"* include writing (alpha) **and** calculation (numeric). Strong's 4284, 2803. Isaiah 28:13; 55:7-10. Jewish *Mitzvots* of Deeds, Words, Thoughts (ordained by God) parallel the Reading, Writing, Arithmetic learning model of Solomon.

[72] Recall the story of Nebachanazar's golden image in the field of Dura (Daniel 3:1)? The Babylonian instruments were tuned to the Pythagorean "serpent" scale whose sound overcame the wicked – a sound revealed to the musicians by the "shinning ones" – the Anaki. *The Shining Ones from Ancient Mesopotamia*, Freedomtek.org. Kappraff, Jay. *The Lost Harmonic Law of the Bible*.

from his (Moses) *mixed multitude*. Among this mixed multitude were the Nephilim and the Anakim – the very giants that introduced Pythagorean tuning ratios and 432hz to mankind on Mt. Hermon– the sound of *Baal*![73]

The Ten Commandments

I am God your Lord …	Do not commit murder
You shall not … images …	Do not commit adultery
Do not take name of God in vain …	Do not steal
Remember the Sabbath Day …	Do not commit perjury
Honor father/mother …	Do not be envious

The Ten Commandments given to Israel on Mt. Sinai were structured via alternation and introversion. "These are the manner in which the tablets were written. Whoever kills a human being was considered to have denied God's existence. Whoever violates the Sabbath is bearing false witness against God the Creator. Adultery is the written parallel to worshipping other gods …"[74]

Man   God

6,7,8,9, 10,5 4,3,2,1

yud   vav   yud

---

[73] The "mixed multitude" that followed Moses out of Egypt included "Nefilim (fallen), **Anakim (giants)**, Giborim (mighty), Refaim (shades), and Amalekites." Yochai. *Zohar*, p. 288.

[74] *The Torah Anthology*, *Book of Shir Hashirim*, Rashi quote p. 187. Rabbi Michael Munk, *The Wisdom in the Hebrew Alphabet* (Mesorah Publications, Ltd., Brooklyn, NY, 2005), p. 59.

The 5th and 10th commandments (*gematria* for Grace and Law respectively) are combined - the first five commandments referring to God, the second five commandments referring to Man - a perfect *these two become one* **chiasm**. This is the **"pattern shown to Moses on the mount!"**[75] This Ten Commandment pattern is a mirror image of the Abrahamic Arithmetic Whole Number Balance of alternation and introversion – the ultimate revelation of spiritual understanding: the Pattern of All created Things ... the Lord's **Seal of Truth**.

It was the God of Israel who ordained righteous music and <u>His</u> equal-temperament tuning all according to <u>His</u> **Seal of Truth**. God on Mt. Sinai heard the sound of the mixed multitude (the Egyptian, Pythagorean, 432hz tuned instruments) and called it the *sound of sorcery*.[76]

Heavy Metal concerts invoke the sound of rebellion, the very sound of the mixed multitude of bygone ages. Scripture goes on to inform us that this mixed multitude all perished in the wilderness – none entered the Holy land of Canaan. Remember that which will *be no more* upon the arrival of The Messiah including idolatry and the music of confusion, sorcery, chaos ... the music of *Baal*.

---

[75] I Chronicles Chapter 28. This is the "pattern" King David told his son Solomon to use to construct the Holy Temple of God.

[76] According to Aaron the High Priest and those who survived the incident of the Golden Calf, the Calf suddenly appeared through Egyptian sorcery and spoke "I am the God of Israel." Not one woman relinquished her gold and silver to the men who worshipped the Golden Calf. This is well recorded in Jewish writings.

The Lord's Angels

The Jewish *Midrash* expounds on the Israelites singing the *Song of Moses* after they arrived on the other side of the Sea of Reeds. According to the Scripture and the Sages, the *singing* of Moses and the Children of Israel preceded the *musicians* who were <u>angels</u>.[77] It is recorded by the famous Romantic pianist and composer, Franz Liszt who visited Chopin at his death bed, that Chopin had euphoric, heavenly visions of <u>angels</u> "singing" the most beautiful music **ON acoustical *instruments* tuned to equal-temperament!!!**[78]

What we <u>see</u> and <u>hear</u> can and will condemn your very soul. Many of the rock "idols" mentioned in this study committed suicide or overdosed on drugs. How many symphonic composers and musicians do you know who were drug addicts, lived a life of sin, were heavily involved in the occult, and took their own life? You rarely hear of any. This study was not written for those accustomed to the sound of rebellion. It was written for those who possess spiritual understanding and love the God of Israel …

Now, let us turn our attention to how the Lord "structures" divinely inspired music using the Pattern of All Things.

---

[77] *Yefeh To'ar*, cited by *Anaf Yosef*, Shemos, Beshalach 23:8. Exodus 15:1-15. Equal-temperament is divinely inspired.

[78] Patrick Kavannaugh. <u>*The Spiritual Lives of Great Composers*</u> (Sparrow Press,1992). "We know that equal-temperament was the tuning system of choice for Chopin's own piano." *Chopin's Revolutionary Legacy: A Pianistic Pianism* by Jon Verbalis.

Structure of Davidic Music

David composed music using the same numerical template he employed to write his Psalms. Remember ... God spoke all things into existence alpha-numerically via text (*praying*, Psalms) and number (*singing*, *Instruments*). The spiritual components of righteous music theory are alternation, introversion, and/or the combination of the two (a *these two become one,* divinely ordained "chiasm" (II Chronicles 5:12-14;7:1-3).

As mentioned earlier in this study, translation, rotation, and reflection transformations are the arithmetic parallels of biblical alternation, introversion, and their unified Identity, the ultimate *chiasm* **1** – a *these two become ONE* "image" of He who created all things.

$$\left[\frac{1}{5}, \, \cdots \, \frac{1}{3}, \, \frac{1}{2}, \, \mathbf{1}, \, \frac{2}{1}, \, \frac{3}{1}, \, \cdots \, \frac{5}{1} \right]$$

The Lord used this *these two become **one*** pattern to create the entire Universe – in the *likeness* of His Name.

Musical Translation

A musical translation is the same thing as repetition or alternation in Scripture. The musical structure above is an example of a glide translation or an alternated repetition.

Musical Reflection

A musical reflection is created when a musical motif is reversed. When a motif is reflected in both horizontally and vertically (rotated), however, the resulting motif is said to be introverted. Thus, when you alternate (translate) and introvert a motif the resulting transformation is called a *chiasm*.

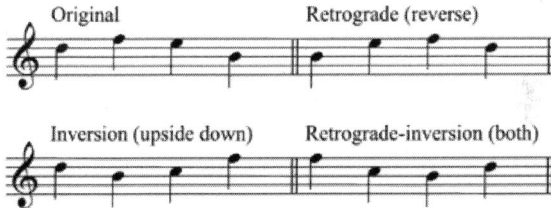

This plate represents a horizontal retrograde (reflection of the original motif) combined with a vertical inversion, called a *chiasm* in Scripture and music. The "original" and "Reverse-inversion" are reciprocals of one another about the note D – an exact copy of the Whole Number Balance (WNB).

There are many musical score combinations you can create using translations, rotations, and reflections of a single musical motif – all of which are structured after the Whole Number Balance of *counting* and *measuring*.

The Whole Number pattern of Alternation and Introversion

COUNT

$$\left[\frac{1}{5}, \ \ldots \ \frac{1}{3}, \ \frac{1}{2}, \ \mathbf{1}, \ \frac{2}{1}, \ \frac{3}{1}, \ \ldots \ \frac{5}{1} \right]$$

← ---------- MEASURE ------------→

A mere image of the Ten Commandment *chiasm* - a "measure" of divine significance – the 10-stringed harp of David.

Translation • Rotation = Reflection

Davidic music is the **transformation** of a musical/biblical motif ... as are all created things in the Universe. Translations represent parallel movement in a melody, whereas, rotations represent perpendicular movement in harmony. When combined, the music of earth parallels or reflects that which is in heaven (perpendicular). Music without horizontal and vertical transformations, however, possess no spiritual component, no reflection of heavenly glory and thus ... cannot bless the *Name* of God.

As you can see, there is more to music (Arithmetic put to three-dimensional sound) than one can imagine. The language of biblical Arithmetic has endured many alterations by the Fathers of Mathematicians and sorcerers of antiquity. One thing these masters of deception overlooked was the *Torah* – the origin of Abrahamic Arithmetic. If music truly is the 49th gate of biblical understanding, then perhaps we should wholeheartedly scrutinize what music we listen to.

A Trial Run

After several years of studying biblical Arithmetic and the Lord's *pattern of all things*, I decided to test the transformational power of its components – namely, translations, rotations, and their combination (the "mentalities" or numerical logic [*mochin*] of the *Zohar*). Johann Sebastian Bach was among the first to incorporate Davidic, *chiastic* structures within his music – a practice that continued throughout the Baroque, Romantic, and Classical eras. Music is the spoken language of transformational, 3-dimensional Arithmetic.

<u>My quest</u>: Would the Spirit of Arithmetic inspire me to compose a song that would lift the spirits of my listeners? That very evening, ... in a dream, a young boy performed a heavenly song for me on the piano!! I woke up ... sat at my piano ... and played the song without flaw! Two weeks later I had finished drafting my first musical score.

Ironically, a week or so after writing the Lord's song, I was invited to perform a piano concert in a local church in Houston, Texas. I arrived at the church prepared to test my composition against the melodies of Beethoven, French composure Fauré, Rachmaninoff, Scott Joplin, Andy Williams, and a variety of other modern composers.

Every person in the audience (around 400 of all ages) received a list of songs I would be performing (10 in all). They were instructed to list the songs in order beginning with the song that "moved their soul the most to the least." I asked them not to mark their responses until after I had finished performing all 10 melodies. Furthermore, I was sure to inform them that I had already marked a list of my own and that, if my experiment was successful, would pre-determine their lists ... then folded and placed my list on the piano.

<u>The challenge</u>: Could I move my listeners to mark their lists according to the melodic structures of each song I performed, placing the composition the Lord revealed to me as close to the top of the list as possible. My selection of melodies included simple and complex structures of alternation, introversion, and their combination.

I completed my performance, opened my list and revealed it to the audience. Most arranged their selections <u>in order of my list</u> placing the Lord's composition **at the top** without having been told the 10 songs included a composition of my own creation. Although I performed the selections well, those without a *chiastic* pattern did not fare as well among the tallies.

The Pastor of the church ran down the aisle and confronted me in front of the audience stating (and I quote): "I do not know what or how you did this, but <u>YOU WILL</u> perform a second concert for the Pastors of Houston and their music Directors." I did so ... and achieved the same results with the most spiritually minded Pastors and accomplished musicians of Houston.

Several of these Pastors were sure to challenge my understanding of Scripture and the "Pattern of All Things." They insisted that I show them where in Scripture they could find the numerical structure I spoke of, especially the WHOLE NUMBER RATIOS themselves. They opened their Bibles and within a few minutes, I satisfied their curiosity. "We and our fathers and grandfathers have studied the Holy Bible all our lives and would have never believed such a numerical pattern existed within the sacred text" was their response.

The Arithmetic, Whole Number balance, by the way, is the arithmetic equivalent of the "these two become one" *Just Balance* of Scripture – the "two-hands" *counting* and *measuring* structure of the Word of God.

According to the *Tanakh*, King David and the prophets received prophetic utterances via instrumental music! The evil spirits that haunted King Saul fled from the sound of David's music. The structure of the Whole Number Balance mirrors the sacred balance of Davidic music, the balance known to Shem and Abraham as the *"Seal of Truth"* – referred to as the *Just Balance* or *Pattern of All Things* in the *Tanakh*. Abraham revealed the rudiments of Arithmetic to the Egyptian and the Greek mathematicians, sorcerers, and astrologers who had no prior knowledge of this divinely inspired language. Most pianos today, by the way, are equal-temperament tuned whose tonal frequency is 440hz.

The frequency structure of equal-temperament music.

$$\left[\frac{1}{5}, \; \dots \; \frac{1}{3}, \; \frac{1}{2}, \; \mathbf{1}, \; \frac{2}{1}, \; \frac{3}{1}, \; \dots \; \frac{5}{1}\right]$$

I am not a concert pianist nor was I ever a professional musician. But ... I **heard** and **saw** the *power* of the *pattern of all things* and its influence on the hearts of those in attendance. Music truly is the spoken language of biblical Arithmetic – a language of divine significance.

I kept my musical score of the Lord's *Impromptu*. This hand-written composition does contain a few errors; nevertheless, I will include it here for your pleasure. I have never had a dream like this since. Fortunately, my wife attended both concerts and can attest to this story.

Blessed be the *name* of HaShem!!!

IMPROMPTU

46

8 basso
mp
Leggiero
simile
rit.
a tempo
ff
con gran espressione

48

simile
allarg.
ff
riten.
a tempo
dim.
accel.
mp
8 bassa
Ped.
Tempo I
ff con gran espressione

poco ritardendo
dim.
sf
mf
Cadenza
crescendo
p
a tempo
ff
8 bassa
mp
leggiero

51

Summary

The Jewish Sages prophesied that in the *end days* very few will be walking a righteous path, for the temptations and spiritual deceptions will be almost impossible to detect or overcome. Who would have thought one of greatest obstacles of divine judgment would be the music we listen to ...... Why not, He created our souls!

I speak on this account of mathematics for the Real Number Scale, the logic of mathematical thought, harbors the very *likeness* and *Spirit* of Pythagorean Tuning (p. 30), the "serpent tuning" system of Egyptian and Greek music used to worship the gods of *Baal*. Is it any wonder that "only 14.6 percent of mathematicians embrace the 'God hypothesis' versus 5.5 percent of biologists."[79] As Enoch stated in the Book of Enoch, the *Spirit* of Mathematics and sorcery is not your friend.[80]

The good Christian should beware of mathematicians and all those who make empty prophesies. The danger already exists that the mathematicians have made a covenant with the devil to darken the spirit and to confine man to the bonds of Hell.[81]

St. Augustine

---

[79] *Irreligion* – John Paulos book review. (www.nytimes.com)
[80] Lumpkin. *The Books of Enoch* (Fifth Estate, 2009), pp. 28,100,108.
[81] Quote redacted from Isaiah 28:15-18.

Sacred Geometry is the Egyptian/Babylonian geometry of ZERO and INFINITY, the geometry of *Baal* worship.[82] All the Eastern religions are religions of Sacred Geometry as are the New Age cults in America. The music of Sacred Geometry glorifies Pythagorean ratios, 432hz, and "spiral of fifths" theories, *Pi*, and the Babylonian Golden Mean – all portents of idolatry and sorcery. All Egyptian, Greek, Hindu Temples, and Notre Dame (sacred abodes of *Pi*, 432, and the Golden Proportion) are Temples dedicated to the SUN-gods of *Baal*. Equal-temperament tuning and chiastic structures are mysteriously absent from Eastern mysticism and for good reason – they do not know the true God of Creation who created sacred, Davidic music.

As I stated at the beginning of this study, Arithmetic and Davidic Music are synonymous terms. So too are Mathematics and the music of *Baal* synonymous terms.[83] To be on the safe side, bless your home with Symphonic, *chiastic* music designed and orchestrated to feed your very soul ... at least Johann Sebastian Bach thought so.

---

[82] The symbolism of sorcery and Sacred Geometry are both derived from Egyptian Mathematics whose sacred icons of idolatry are ZERO and INFINITY ... the very icons and symbolism of Calculus. *Thoth*, the Egyptian "Father of Intelligence and Mathematics" (and Sacred Geometry) was identified with the SUN-god *Baal* and the Greek Hermes. Ions, Veronica. *Egyptian Mythology* (New York: Peter Bedrick Books, 1968), pp. 84, 85. I expound of this subject in my book *The Seal of Truth*.

[83] I speak of mathematical symbolism, Zero, infinite measures, and the false Time/Space of scientific nonsense. Abrahamic Arithmetic, by the way, is unknown in the field of Modern Mathematics.

The Zohar

The *Zohar*, referred to as the *Hidden Torah*, was first introduced by Abraham (also the author of biblical Arithmetic). The *Zohar* is not the Theoretical Kabbalah we have today, but the Classical Kabbalah of Abraham written in a *text* format. All things of God, however, are alpha-numeric (of *text* and *number*). The *numerical* counterpart to the *Zohar,* emphatically, is biblical Arithmetic – a language forgotten many years ago until recently rediscovered – the only Hebraic "language" that bears witness to the *Zohar* – a language extracted directly from the *Torah*.

The *Zohar* is a mystical work whose sacred symbolism have been transliterated here for your understanding - in particular, the section on spiritual music. To scrutinize synonymous terminology, only the words of the *Zohar* are **bold** and ***italicized***. The remaining *italicized* parallels are taken directly from the *Torah*. We begin with a list of synonymous *Zohar/Torah/Arithmetic* terminology.

Synonymous Terms

The IDENTITY of Whole Number Arithmetic is the numeral **1**, good ***Mochin*** of the Kabbalistic *Cochmah*, and the **Holy ONE** in the Torah.

The IDENTITY of Real Number Mathematics is the numeral **0**, *evil **Mochin*** of the Zohar, the *scant measure* of the Tanakh whose biblical parallels include *False Weight*, *Nothing*, and *Death*.

The WHOLE NUMBER BALANCE (WNB) of Arithmetic is called ***Malkhut of Holiness*** or the rectified *Line of Righteousness* in the Zohar, a balance of *comely proportion* called the **Just Balance** or *pattern of all things* in the Tanakh, and a **chiasm** in music.

The REAL NUMBER BALANCE (RNB) of Mathematics is called the **Malkhut of the Other Side** in the Zohar, the unrectified *Line of Confusion* of *infinite iniquities* in the Tanakh and referred to by Job and Isaiah as the *False Balance* or *Hell*.

Mochin is the **these two become one** motif or mentalities ("inner intelligence") of the Zohar and the Kabbalist Tree of Life, the "logic" (reciprocity or opposites) of the WNB and RNB in Arithmetic and Mathematics respectively, and the *these two become one Seal of Truth* (*Tav*) in the Torah.

Voice is referred to in the Zohar as spoken *word or praying*, referred to as *word*, *Wisdom,* or *Psalm* in the Tanakh, as "1" in Arithmetic, and the "tonal frequency" in music.

Speech is referred to in the Zohar as *singing*, referred to as *Understanding*, *Hymn*, *Number*, *Measure*, and *Instruments* in the Tanakh, as the "WNB" in Arithmetic (or the *scant measure* of the "RNB" in Mathematics), and as *octave* in music.

Song is the combination of *Voice* and *Speech* in the Zohar, the combination of *Psalm* and *instruments* in the Tanakh, and the combination of *Translation* and *Reflection* in Arithmetic and Music (called a "chiasm"). *Speech* and *musical Instruments* are divine implements of *Prophecy* (Song).

These terms by no means exhaust the similarities between the disciplines *Torah, Zohar,* and *Arithmetic.* They are, nevertheless, sufficient to distinguish and recognize the differences between righteous (good) and wicked (evil) music.

The Identities (**mochin**) of the two **Malkhuts** (of Holiness and of the Other Side) encompasses the totality of the intelligence or "structure" of **Malkhut**. The **mochin** of the **Malkhut of Holiness** is restricted – has boundaries on one's intellect. The **mochin** of the **Malkuht of the Other Side** has no boundaries (infinite) motivated by personal gain, great wealth, honor, and fame. These attributes associated with **mochin** and the two paths of **Malkhut** corresponds word for word with the Whole Number Balance and the Real Number Balance respectively.

The Malkhut of Holiness
The Whole Number Balance (WNB) called the *Just Balance* in Scripture

$$[\frac{1}{5}, \; ... \; \frac{1}{3}, \; \frac{1}{2}, \; \mathbf{1}, \; \frac{2}{1}, \; \frac{3}{1}, \; ... \; \frac{5}{1}]$$

The Malkhut of the Other Side
The Real Number Balance (RNB) called the *False Balance* in Scripture

$$-\infty ... \; -3, \; -2, -1, \; \mathbf{0}, +1, +2, +3 \; ...+\infty$$

No Beginning and End (*Alef* and *Tav*) to Time, all is Big Bang.

The Identity 1 of the WNB contains all arithmetic ratios of the WNB (as does **Cochkmah** and its balance **Binah** in *Zohar* terminology). This "restricted" balance, referred to as the *Pattern of All Things* in the *Torah*, employs the frequencies of the equal-tempered scale and all the color ratios of the rainbow[84] as does the "**All**" of **Yoshed** – a key element in the "intellectual" structure of the **Malkhut of Holiness** (and the Kabbalist *Tree of Life*) - that of alternation, introversion, and their combination.

All measures of *Torah* and the *Zohar*, including the **Malkhut of Holiness**, are a *these two become one* pattern of measure three. The "mentalities" of the **mochin** are

---

[84] The **mochin** of the WNB is *reciprocity;* whereas the **mochin** of the RNB is *division of opposites*. The **Malkhut of Holiness** received light from its **mochin** as does the WNB receive light from the Unit Builder 1 whose measure is the very electromagnetic measure of visible Light! The **Malkhut of the Other Side** receives darkness from its **mochin** as does the *infinite iniquities* of the RNB and is referred to as *Death* and *Hell* (Isaiah 28:15-18) in the Jewish Scriptures.

grouped in threes[85] as are all biblical, arithmetic mentalities of alternation, introversion, and the "combination of the two." The Jewish Scriptures are ordered according to the arithmetic, whole number *pattern of all things*, a *these two become one* pattern of alternation and introversion of parts (the "mentality" or "intellect" of the *Jewish Scriptures*).

The Real Number Balance of Mathematics, however, is an unrectified balance of opposites (called a balance of ***"dispute"*** in the *Zohar*), an unrestricted balance the Lord counts as *nothing, less than nothing, and vanity* (Isaiah 40:17,18). So too is the structure of the Zohar's **Malkhut of the Other Side** an unrestricted balance of vanity.

Song

Using the synonymous terminology, let us compare the mentalities (logic) of the *Zohar,* as they relate to song, with the intellectual structure of the *Torah*.[86]

Zohar
Voice • Speech = SONG

Torah
Psalm • Instruments = SONG

---

[85] Rebbe Nachmann, <u>Likutey Moharan</u> (Breslov Research Institute, Jerusalem, 2012), p.42. There are three columns to the Kabbalistic Tree of Life. The Three Mothers or *mochin* of Kabbalah are <u>text</u>, <u>number</u>, and <u>their combination</u> – an arithmetic mochin.

[86] The symbol "•" in the *Zohar* (<u>Likutey Moharan</u>, p.34) and *Torah* refers to multiplication – a *these two reciprocal parts become ONE* by the power of multiplication.

Wisdom [word] • Understanding [number] = Knowledge is the biblical pattern the Lord established to structure all things including music.[87] According to the *Zohar*, "when listening to singing of the wicked his **voice** is blemished and exposed to the ***Malkhut of the Other Side***.[88] *Speech* or music without reciprocity (***Malkhut of the Other Side***) does not rectify **voice** [does not glorify the *Name* of God][89] ... what the *Zohar* calls ***"evil mochin* or *speech."***

The biblical *Just Balance* or WNB, a balance of reciprocity, is referred to in the *Zohar* as a "balance of rectified disputes."[90] Reciprocal ratios of the WNB [i.e. 2/1 and 1/2], when multiplied equal **1**. Rectification, using either *Torah* or *Zohar* terminology, is accomplished via alternation and introversion of parts, and the combination of both[91] - the biblical *these two become* **ONE** inner intelligence of the *Zohar*, the *Torah,* and its

---

[87] The Hebraic and Greek definition of "Word" is "text [word] and calculation [number]." Kabbalist Aryeh Kaplan in his <u>Sefer Yetzirah</u> identifies three books (text, number, and their combination) the Lord uses to communicate all things to man and man to God.

[88] Ibid. p.98. This corresponds with the Jewish *Midrash*: "intelligence and understanding is greater than wisdom (text, **voice**) because understanding (number, **speech**) comes from the **mouth** of God." <u>Midrash</u>, Ki Sisam 41:3. ***Malkhut*** and ***speech*** correspond to **mouth**. Biblical knowledge, as in the ***Zohar***, is predicated upon understanding (***speech***) - Arithmetic and its WNB.

[89] There is no rectification in real number logic (i.e. $2 \cdot (-2) \neq 1$).

[90] Rev Simon bar Yochai, <u>Zohar</u> (New York, NY, 2003), p. 180.

[91] The three columns of the Kabbala Tree of Life represent alteration (left side), introversion (right side) and the combination of both (the central column).

Seal of Truth[92] whose biblical *way* and *path* is *life* and *light* respectively.

The compositional structures of Rock Music are completely void of reciprocity, of alternation, introversion, and their combination ... *chiasms* – the biblical components of righteous, Davidic music. Both the *Torah* and the *Zohar* confirm this. You compound this issue if you tune your unrectified composition to Pythagorean and Just Intonation ratios (which do not conform to equal-temperament ratios) and adopt the Anaki "tonal frequency" of 432hz!

The *Zohar* further states that when the left column of the Kabbalah Tree of Life "is aroused, its dispute with the right column began and the fire of anger in that dispute became fierce. Gehenom (Hell) was awakened, <u>created by the left</u>, and cleaved to it."[93] The Unit Builder of the *False Balance* (the false "whole number" ZERO) and its biblical *way* and *path* is referred to as "Death and Hell" both in the *Tanakh* and the *Zohar* (Isaiah 28:15-18).

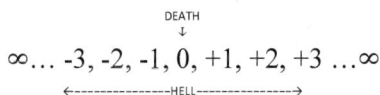

$$\infty... -3, -2, -1, 0, +1, +2, +3 ...\infty$$

DEATH ↓ ... ←------------HELL------------→

---

[92] Rabbi Aaron Raskin, *Letters of Light* (New York), p. 221-3.

[93] *Zohar*, p. 180. In both the Hebrew Scriptures and the *Zohar*, the left column is the origin of all disputes (no "reciprocity" with the right). In other words, the measuring mechanism (left side) of Rock Music is evil – *You are counted as <u>nothing</u> [Zero], You are <u>less than nothing</u> [negative], your effect is less than nullity; One who chooses your [music of idolatry] is an abomination (Isaiah 40:15-17; 41:24).*

The universal "pattern" of rectification, of which all things of vibration, light, sound, and crystalline structure, are created, is in the "likeness"[94] of the Whole Number Balance.[95] The Whole Number Balance is a balance of convergence – a convergence to 1, the Holy ONE of rectification. The Real Number Balance diverges to infinite chaos (no restrictions or reciprocity). The Tree of Good and Evil corresponds to the **Maklhut of Holiness** (good) and the **Malkhut of the Other Side** (evil).

The *Tanakh* and the *Zohar* both associate <u>*good*</u> with the Right Hand of Glory, whereas, <u>*evil*</u>, what Isaiah described as *nothing (biblical ZERO), less than nothing (negative numbers), and vanity (INFINITE Time or decimals)*, with the Left Hand of Judgment. Notice that ZERO and INFINITY (∞), the numerical icons of Calculus, Egyptian Sacred Geometry, and the idolatrous mandalas of Eastern religions, <u>reside on the wrong Hand</u>![96] Two things that will cease to exist upon the arrival of The Messiah are idolatry and the **music** of idolatry! Amen.

> *The heart (understanding) of a wise man is to his right, and the heart of a fool is to his left.*[97]

---

[94] The structure of the Whole Number Balance is the **structure of reality** in the *likeness* of the Creator. Strong's 1823. Genesis 1:26.

[95] Review the Goldschmidt Series on pages 26, 27. "There exists an invariant, universal tonal scale of which "any scale (of natural frequencies) can be represented geometrically." And ... that scale is the whole number scale of Abrahamic Arithmetic.

[96] "The Messiah will judge by smell. The left side of the Messiah's nose is reserved for judgment. " *Likutey Moharan*, p.52.

[97] *Torah Anthology*, The Book of Koheleth:10,2; p. 231.

Summary List of Parallels

Torah

Aleph	Tav	Seal of Truth
Wisdom	Understanding	Knowledge
Father	Holy Spirit	God (Holy ONE)
Alternation	Introversion	Chiasm
Body	Spirit	Soul
Psalm	Instrument	Song
Count	Measure	All Things
Name (*alpha*)	Number (*numeric*)	Word
Sabbath	Festivals	Calendar
Written Law	Oral Law	Will of God
Words	Thoughts	Deeds

Zohar

Chokhmah	Binah	Daat
Gevurah	Chesed	Tiferet
Hod	Netzach	Yesod
Text	Number	Communication
Voice	Speech	Malkhut

New Testament

6 (for count)	*666* (for measure)	**Beast** (for *Trinity*)

Science

Translation	Rotation	Reflection
Electricity	Magnetism	Light
Green	Purple	White
Arithmetic Mean	Harmonic Mean	Geometric Mean
Adenine	Thymine	DNA
Time	Space	Universe
Proton	Electron	Neutron

Arithmetic

Writing	Arithmetic	Reading
1	WNB	Arithmetic

All these parallels are a *these two become one* pattern of alternation and introversion. Everything the Lord created including the Holy Scriptures is in His *likeness* of *these two **become one*** (with the exception of *Baal*, Paul's *these three **are** one* god of iniquity).

61

Hebrew Glossary

HaShem: In Judaism, HaShem (lit. "the Name") is **used to refer to as the God of mercy, particularly as an epithet for the Tetragrammaton, when avoiding God's more formal title, Adonai ("my master")**. Elohim refers to the God of Judgment.

Midrash: In its broadest sense, Midrash is **interpretation of any text**; in its strictest sense, it designates rabbinic biblical interpretation, the modes of exegesis, as well as specific corpora of rabbinic literature from Antiquity to the early medieval period.

Jewish Sage: Sages are identified as **wisdom teachers who provide their pupils with models for living.** A list of sages includes Hillel, Shammai, Rabbi Akiba, Judah Ha-Nasi, Rashi, Maimonides, Rebbe Nachman of Breslov, and the Baal Shem Tov.

Seal of Truth: The combination of the *Aleph* and *Tav* form a pattern in the *likeness* of the biblical Pattern of All Things. *Aleph* (1) is to cardinal numeration as the *Tav* is to ordinal numeration. The letter *Tav* (ת) is composed of **1,2,3** lines (measures) and a *Yud* (י) or point, the Unit Builder ONE of the WNB of which emanates all numeration.

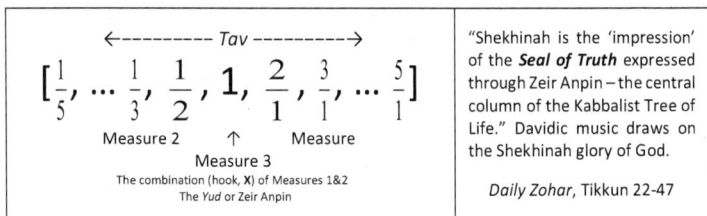

←--------- *Tav* ---------→ $$\left[\frac{1}{5}, \dots \frac{1}{3}, \frac{1}{2}, 1, \frac{2}{1}, \frac{3}{1}, \dots \frac{5}{1}\right]$$ Measure 2　↑　Measure Measure 3 The combination (hook, **X**) of Measures 1&2 The *Yud* or Zeir Anpin	"Shekhinah is the 'impression' of the **Seal of Truth** expressed through Zeir Anpin – the central column of the Kabbalist Tree of Life." Davidic music draws on the Shekhinah glory of God. *Daily Zohar*, Tikkun 22-47

Talmud: The Talmud is the central text of Rabbinic Judaism and the primary source of Jewish religious law and Jewish theology - the Oral Law given on Mt. Sinai.

Tanakh: The Hebrew Bible or Tanakh, also known in Hebrew as Miqra, is the canonical collection of Hebrew scriptures, including the Torah, the Nevi'im (Prophets), and the Ketuvim (Writings).

Torah: The Torah is the compilation of the first five books of the Hebrew Bible, namely the books of Genesis, Exodus, Leviticus, Numbers and Deuteronomy. In that sense, Torah means the same as Pentateuch or the Five Books of Moses. It is also known in the Jewish tradition as the Written Torah.

Zohar: The Zohar, the "Hidden Torah," is a foundational work in the literature of Jewish mystical thought known as Kabbalah. It is a group of books including commentary on the mystical aspects of the Torah and scriptural interpretations as well as material on mysticism, mythical cosmogony, and mystical psychology.

Mitzvot: Good deeds.

Appendix

All the people <u>saw</u> the thunderings, and the lightnings, and the noise of the trumpet, and the mountain smoking; and when the people saw it, they removed, and stood afar off. [98]

This Appendix is added to assist your understanding of Exodus 20:18 KJ (Exodus 20:15, MT) and its relevance to "the <u>structure</u> and the <u>sound</u> of Davidic music." Hebrew letters came forth from the sound of the trumpets. Those in attendance at Mt. Sinai *saw* and *heard* these letters, letters that spoke to Israel! The Hebrew Prophets also *saw* these letters when their minstrels played on their instruments and communicated with them audibly. [99]

The entire Hebrew alphabet is contained within the first letter in the alphabet – the *Aleph*. All counting and measuring numbers are also contained within the *Aleph*. The structure of the letter *Aleph*, is one of alternation, introversion, and their combination – a *chiastic* structure. The universe was structured according to the *image* and *likeness* of this letter called the *Seal of Truth*. Not only did the people of Mt. Sinai *see* the א and its structure ב, they also *heard* the sound that came forth from them. The arithmetic equivalents of א and ב are 1 and WNB whose combination represents the frequencies of both the *light* (**saw**) and the *sound* (**heard**) spectra.

---

[98] Me'Am Lo'Ez, *The Torah Anthology* (Moznaim Publishing Corp., New York, 1990), p. 133.
[99] II Kings 3:15.

The Hebrew letter *Aleph* represents ONE – the beginning of all counting and measuring. Notice that the two *Yuds* (points) are <u>alternated and introverted</u> about *Vav* creating a bounded line of 5 and 5. Recall Isaiah 28:13 and Euclid's point, line, plane and compare what you know about the *Aleph* and the PAT:

Count

$$\left[\frac{1}{5}, \ldots \frac{1}{3}, \frac{1}{2}, \mathbf{1}, \frac{2}{1}, \frac{3}{1}, \ldots \frac{5}{1}\right]$$

|---------------------------Measure---------------------------|

Does the construction of the *Aleph* allow for the division of the *Yud* into 5 and 5 (as is the 10 Commandments) bearing reciprocal relationships (as within the reciprocal relationships between commandments 1-5 and 6-10)? Set aside gematria for a moment and consider the numerical, counting and measuring aspect of the alpha-<u>numeric</u> language of Hebrew. The *Aleph* not only is the beginning and end of all that is written, it is also the first and last of all that is counted and measured. **Also, the two-HANDS counting system of antiquity is an exact copy of this *Aleph* motif.**

Hebrew is, indeed, a "living" language. Do not let anyone deceive you in thinking Hebrew is not the divine language of God and Creation. The Lord chose Hebrew to reveal Himself to mankind and created the entire universe with the Hebrew letters *Aleph* and *Bet* – a *these two [א* and *ב] became one* Creation. The only way you will ever learn about the God of Israel, His people, and righteous Gentiles is through the *Torah*. Davidic music was ordained to reveal this message to your very soul. May the Lord bless you and your family.   Amen.

The Shofar

When on Mt. Sinai, the sound of the ram's horn spoke saying **"I am God your Lord,"** all the Gentile nations also **saw** (in their own languages) this sound![100] Stop and consider what the Lord is saying here. When you play instruments, you hear the *sound*, but only the soul hears the *words*. Music speaks to the soul, literally! So, be careful what music you and your children listen to, and remember, you will be judged as to what music you feed your soul. Upon the sound of the *Last Great Shofar*, your eternal destiny will be sealed.

---

[100] *The Torah Anthology*, Exodus III, p. 32.